This library edition published in 2015 by Walter Foster Jr.,
a division of Quarto Publishing Group USA Inc.
3 Wrigley, Suite A
Irvine, CA 92618

Distributed in the United States and Canada by
Lerner Publisher Services
241 First Avenue North
Minneapolis, MN 55401 U.S.A.
www.lernerbooks.com

First Library Edition

Library of Congress Cataloging-in-Publication Data

Winterberg, Jenna.
  Outer space / Story by Jenna Winterberg ; Illustrations by Diana Fisher. -- Library edition.
      pages cm. -- (Watch me draw)
  ISBN 978-1-93958-135-8
  1. Outer space--In art--Juvenile literature. 2. Drawing--Technique--Juvenile literature. I. Fisher, Diana (Diana L.), illustrator. II. Title.
   NC825.O9W56 2015
   743'.8--dc23
                                                                    2013011683

012015
18582

9 8 7 6 5 4 3 2 1

Outer Space

Story by Jenna Winterberg • Illustrations by Diana Fisher

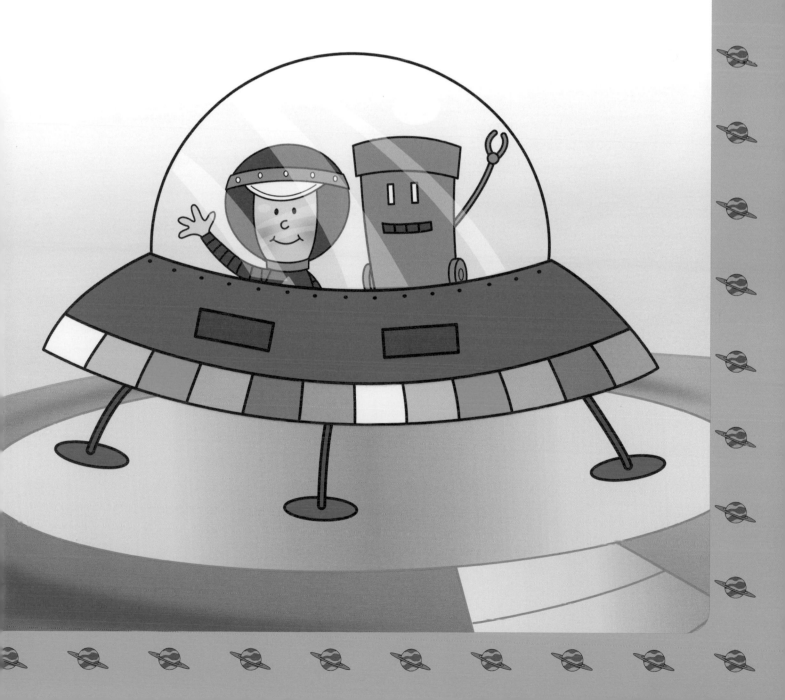

"Sparky! Sparky, where are you?" Atom, a young alien boy, has been calling his pup for a full half an hour, but Sparky isn't responding. Atom already tried looking all the usual places—under his bed, in the craters behind his house, even in his dad's spacepod. Just where in the galaxy could his little dog be?

Draw Atom the alien boy!

Atom is sure that Sparky hasn't run away. But his puppy could be lost in space somewhere. He imagines his little dog, cold and alone. He has to rescue Sparky! Atom gathers his space helmet, a star map, and an astronaut snack—just in case. Then he calls out to his telescope, "Telly, I need your help!"

Draw Telly the telescope!

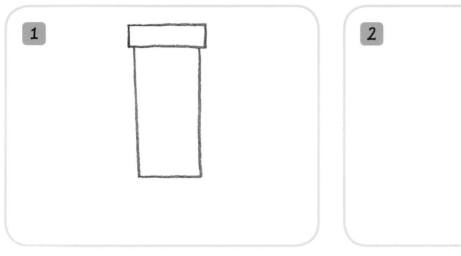

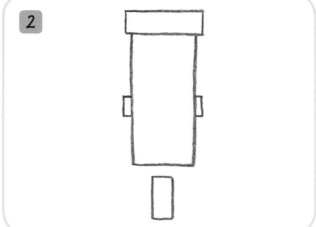

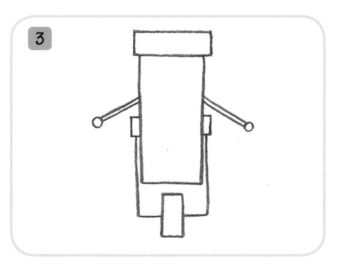

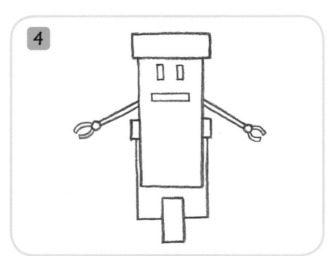

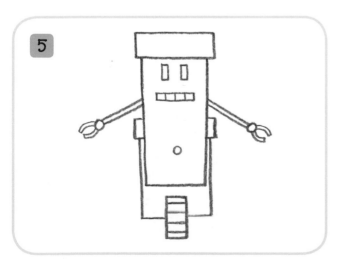

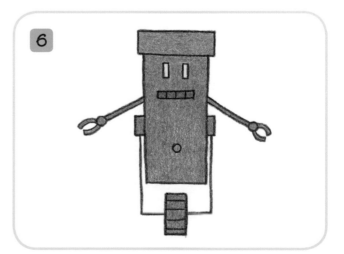

Telly rolls toward Atom. "Telly," says Atom, "Sparky is lost. But I'm sure he's wearing his radio collar." Atom Knows that Elle, the satellite, can track radio signals anywhere in the universe. "If we can find Elle, we can find Sparky, wherever he is!" Atom exclaims. When Atom peers through Telly's scope, sure enough, he spots Elle!

Draw Elle the satellite!

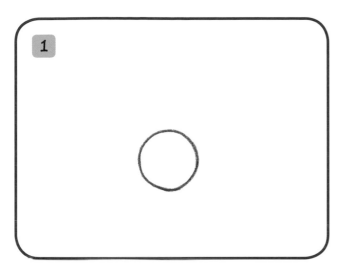

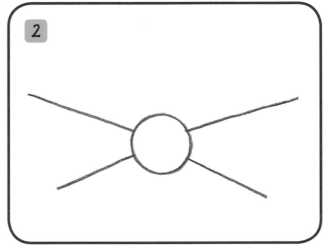

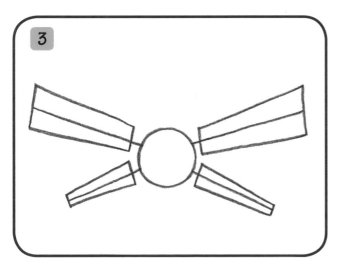

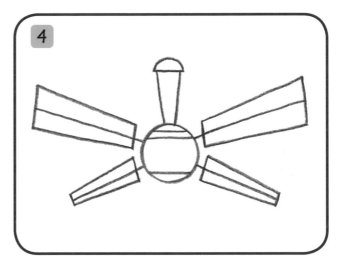

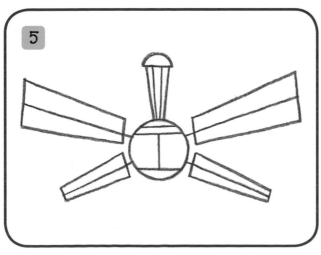

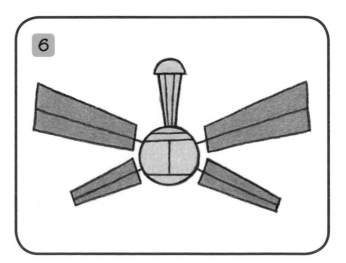

Now Atom thinks aloud, "What's the quickest way to get to Elle?" Then he remembers riding the rocket ship to school each day. "I know— Rod can take us!" Atom runs toward the rocket stop, with Telly following closely behind him. When the two arrive at the launch pad, Rod, the rocket ship, is waiting for the okay to lift off.

Draw Rod the rocket ship!

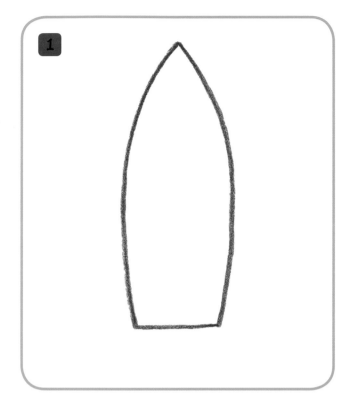

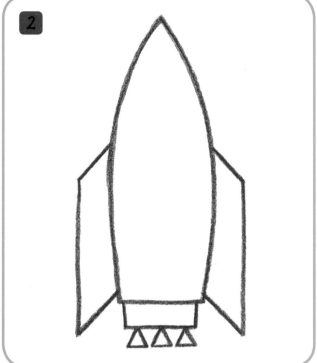

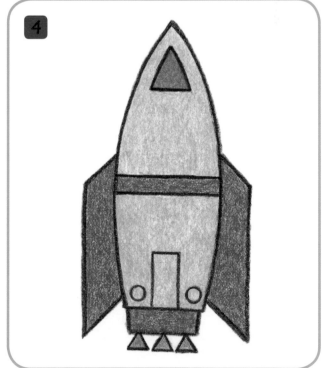

Rod says hello to Atom and encourages him to hurry. "The countdown's about to start," Rod warns. Atom and Telly quickly find window seats and fasten their safety belts. A moment later, the ship rockets into space. Atom spots a comet through the glass, and Telly helps him take a closer look. "Sparky sure would like to see that," sighs Atom.

Draw the comet!

1

2

3

4

When the rocket lands, Atom puts on his helmet. Then he and Telly step down onto the surface of the satellite. But it isn't until Rod speeds away that Atom discovers Elle is closed for repairs! "Now how will we find Sparky?" wonders Atom. But Telly is already one step ahead: He points at a nearby planet surrounded by satellites!

Draw the planet!

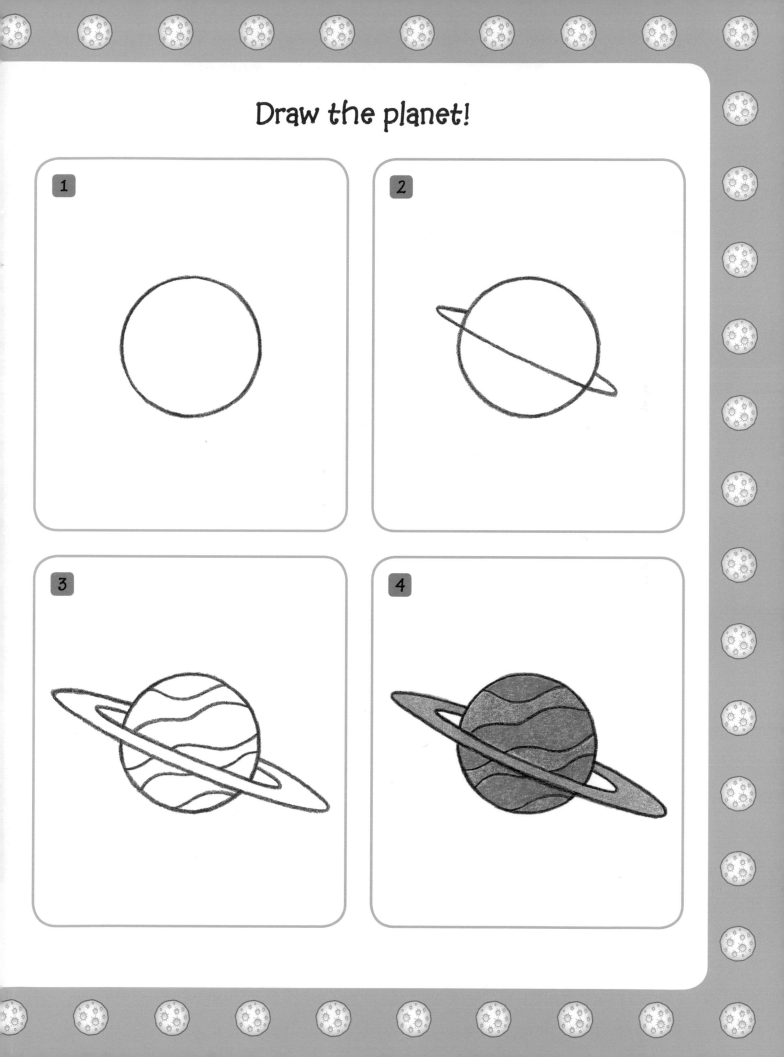

"A planet with so many satellites can definitely tune in to Sparky's signal!" shouts Atom. But his excitement quickly becomes disappointment. "It's so far away, though. How are we going to get there?" A nearby star provides the answer. "Allow me to offer my services. I'm Twinkle, with Shooting Star Transport."

Draw Twinkle the star!

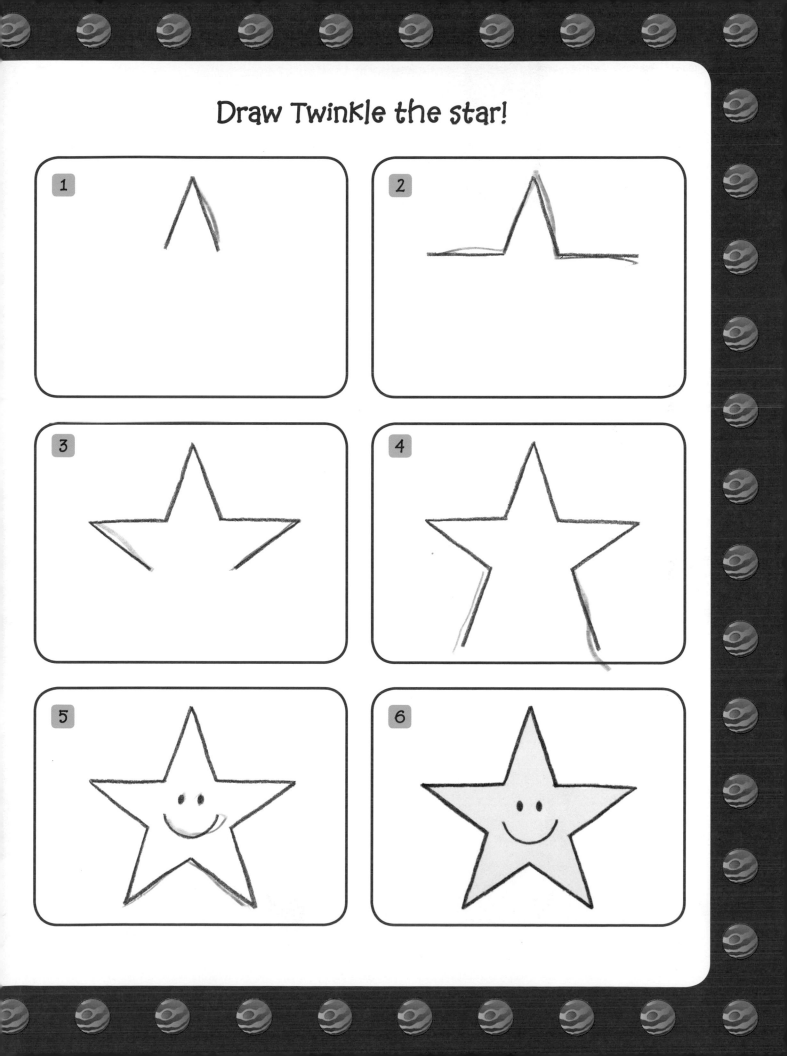

Talk about thanking your lucky stars! Not only would they get to the planet, they'd get to ride on a shooting star in the process! In a twinkle, the star transports the two friends safely to the planet's surface, where Rover, the space vehicle, is waiting. "We need a satellite to locate a signal," Atom quickly tells Rover. "Sparky, here we come!"

Draw Rover the space vehicle!

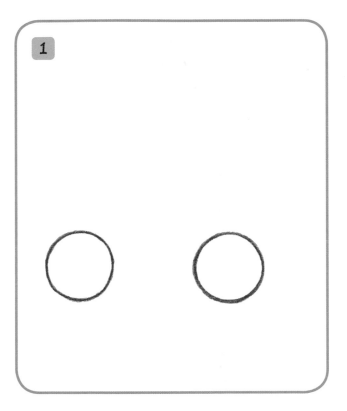

But Rover tells Atom that the objects orbiting the planet aren't satellites—they're moons! And moons won't help Atom find Sparky. "Don't worry," says Rover, "I know who can help." Rover takes the pair to an amazing space palace. They come face to face with Crater, the space mutant!

Draw Crater the space mutant!

"Rover," whispers Atom, staring at Crater, "I'm a little nervous." Rover smiles and nudges Atom forward. Cautiously, Atom asks Crater for help. And, to Atom's surprise, Crater kindly offers the use of his personal UFO! "You can find Sparky's radio signal and fly to his rescue," Crater says.

Draw the UFO!

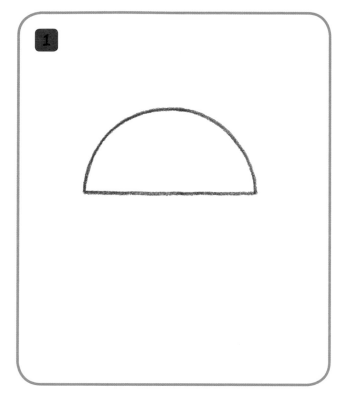

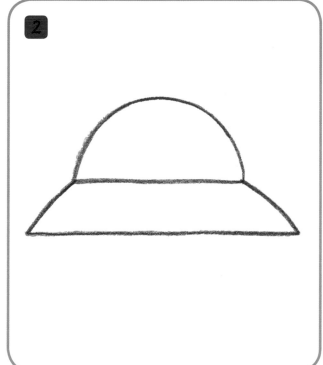

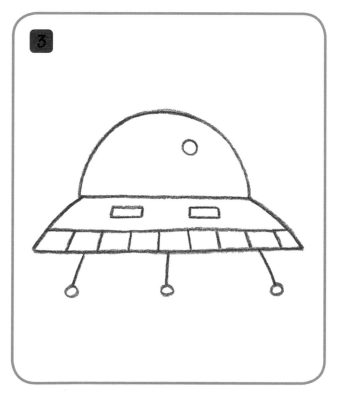

In the UFO, Atom turns on his radio belt to locate Sparky's signal. But he's surprised by an incoming message—from his mom! "Sparky's back from his recharge at the vet," she says. "The vet," Atom moans, "Sparky's not missing after all!" The UFO rushes Atom home, where Sparky waits with a wagging tail. "Oh, Sparky," says Atom, "have I got a story to tell you!"

Draw Sparky the robot dog!

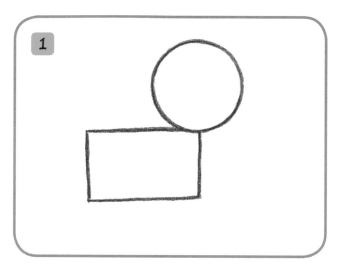

The end.